Book Publication Data:

Isaacs, Tannis

We are Healthy! We are well!

Children's Education, Health, Nutrition

First Printing July 2022

Printed in The United States of America

Dedicated to one of my greatest teachers, who inspires me to overcome the fears that block my potential, my beautiful son, Josiah.

Love,
Mommy

Jamir : I don't know

Ryan : OOH! I KNOW! I KNOW!

      you eat foods that help your body grow!

01

Josiah : PINEAPPLES.

Somaya : PEARS, BANANAS.

Andrew : TOMATOES, AVOCADOS, WATERMELONS.

Jamir : CUCUMBERS, BEETS, GREENS! Anything that comes from a tree!

**We Are Healthy
We Are Well**

Ms.Green : How do you feel when you eat healthy food?

Zayna : Healthy food helps your mood while bad food gives you an attitude.

Logan : It makes you feel really good inside.

Josiah : Fruits and vegetables have good vibes.

05

Somaya : Did you know that if you eat healthy
you will live to be 105 years old!

Emily : Hey! That's not true!
You will only live to be 102!

Class : We know! We know what rhymes with the word "dandy"!

THAT'S CANDY !

Josiah : But it can't be bad because it makes us happy when we're sad.

11

**We Are Healthy
We Are Well**

Ms. Green : That's true, some unhealthy foods make us feel good, but we should not eat them as often as we could. Can we name some more?

Jamir : CHIPS, DONUTS, CAKES, COOKIES, ICE CREAM, SUGAR, BACON !

Ryan : What's wrong with bacon?

Jamir : I don't know but I heard my mom say, too much of it isn't good. Is that true?

Zayna : You will get sick and have a tummy ache!

Logan : Your brain will feel groggy, and you know
what else? You will get a cavity!

15

We Are Healthy We Are Well

Ms. Green : Okay! So, do we all agree that eating unhealthy food isn't good for us?

16

Class : YES !

17

Josiah : Everything on the list except for the thing that rhymes with candy.

Logan : But fruits also taste like candy.

Emily: YOGA.

Somaya: WALKING.

Josiah: EXERCISE.

Logan: SLEEPING.

Zayna : MEDITATION.

22

Jamir : EVERYTHING THAT IS CLEAN! That's

what I think wellness means.

Ryan : BEING OUTSIDE IN NATURE!

Jamir : It means taking care of yourself so that

you can take care of your mom, dad,

brother, sister, and your dog!

23

Check out these Health and Wellness Tips!

Eat your colors at every meal! Your food should be red, purple, green, yellow, orange, and blue! These foods are healthy and yummy too!

Red:

Purple:

Green:

Yellow:

Orange:

Do you have a favorite juice that you like to drink?
How about you eat the fruit instead of drinking the
juice. Your energy will sharply increase! It has less sugar
too! Doesn't that sound healthier to you?

Strawberry

Watermelon

Grapefruit

Plum

Banana

Orange

Blueberry

☐

- Water is better to quench your thirst!

☐

- Water gives you an energy burst!

☐

- Water puts you in a good mood!

☐

- Water gives you the energy to help your body move!

☐

- Water can cool your body down when it gets too hot!

Don't believe me! Give it a shot!

28

When you want something to do try these on! Wellness will look good on you!

_____

Wellness Checklist

☐

· Go outside and play.

☐

· Explore a nature trail.

☐

· Write a letter to someone you love.

☐

· Practice yoga.

☐

· Read your favorite books.

☐

· Take a nap.

☐

· Practice meditation.

☐

· Draw a picture.

☐

· Cook a meal with your family.

About the Author:

Tannis Isaacs is the owner of Tee's Plant Base Kitchen, where she specializes in Caribbean Fusion Plant Base Cuisine. As a Proud Guyanese, Tannis loves to fuse her favorite recipes from her native country Guyana, and neighboring Caribbean countries to create innovative and delicious plant-based dishes that delight and surprise her customers. Most recently, Tannis has the title of "Certified Health & Wellness Coach" to her resume. With her evolving knowledge, she is committed to empowering women and families with the tools that they need to make their wellness a priority and become the optimal version of themselves.

Out of all the titles, Tannis holds her favorite one by far is "Mommy" as she is the mother to a beautiful dynamic six-year-old son Josiah. In her free time, Tannis enjoys cooking with her son and mother who is a professionally trained chef. She also enjoys being outdoors exploring nature and hiking.

Thank you for purchasing my first book. Writing a book has always been a dream for me and now it has finally been manifested. As you can imagine this is an exciting time in my life. It has been a pleasure to share with you something that I am so passionate about, which is health and wellness

This book was also inspired by conversations that my son and I have surrounding nutrition. I hope this book inspires you and your family to find fun and creative ways to incorporate more healthy foods and play that encourages wellness.

Let's keep in touch! follow me on Instagram at:

www.instagram.com/tannis_isaacs

Made in United States
North Haven, CT
20 November 2022